7 Day Spring Cleaning

Make your Place Shining Spending Only 30 Minutes a Day!

LINDA HAYDEN

TABLE OF CONTENT

INTRODUCTION

Everybody looks forward to the coming of spring. Well, everybody who doesn't have to do spring cleaning, that is.

Spring cleaning is more than just a tradition. Yes, some people do this because they used to do it with their parents back when they were still small. It is something that they grew up doing and now has taken roots in their annual list of things to do.

Spring cleaning is an opportunity for a fresh start. It is just like following your New Year's resolution in January. With the cold weather on its way out, you can open your doors and windows and allow the warmth and cleansing properties of the sunlight to come in again.

With people's lives getting more and more hectic each day, a lot of us may have neglected our homes for quite some time.

The changes don't happen overnight. One day, you leave a book on the coffee table. After a few days, you leave another one there. Over time, your coffee table is no longer visible under all the books, bills, flyers, restaurant menus, and other things that shouldn't be there in the first place.

You look at it and decide that you don't have the energy to deal with it, so you just let the clutter sit there. With the coming of spring and the warmth coming back, you should take advantage of the extra energy that it brings you by dealing with all the home upkeep that you have neglected for weeks.

"There are so many chores to do! I don't want to slave away all day inside the house when the weather is so great outside." That's logical. But, if you start your spring cleaning a bit earlier, you will be done by the time the weather gets truly warm. Plus, this book will help you plan your cleaning schedule, so you don't have to "slave away all day". All you need is half an hour (or a few hours, depending on how bad the home situation is) for one week to go through all the tasks that you will need to do in order to put your entire house back in order.

The book starts off by providing you with the motivation and the list of things that you will need in order to make your spring-cleaning project a success. You are then given a list of tasks that you can tick off one by one. You will need to go through one room at a time. By the end of the week, your entire home will be ready to welcome the coming of spring.

Chapter 1 – Getting Ready to Clean

While everybody can benefit from doing spring cleaning, not everyone looks forward to doing this chore. There are some things that you can do to psyche yourself up. The first thing to do is to look at what you are getting back. Nothing can boost your motivation for doing something by looking at the benefits of doing it. The next step is to get all your supplies and task list in order. Once you know that you have everything on hand, it will be easier to push yourself to go through your plan.

The Relevance of Spring Cleaning

Spring cleaning is an old practice that has been carried over into our time. Back in the day, people hunkered down every winter. Fires were lit in order to heat the homes. Because there was no insulation before, household owners kept everything tightly closed to keep the cold air out and the warmth in. This led to an accumulation of grime and soot on pretty much everything. That is why people had to do a lot of cleaning once the snow started melting.

While some modern homes still have fireplaces, most houses are equipped with furnaces, heat pumps, and other heating technologies. This means it is no longer necessary to do a thorough cleaning once spring comes around. So, why do so many people still do spring cleaning? It is not just because we had gotten used to doing it. It is also because there are actual benefits to doing a deep cleaning of the house every year.

Spring Cleaning Can Boost Your Productivity

So, you are ready to do some gardening after a long time of staying inside. You want to get rid of the weeds that surreptitiously grew under all that snow. You need your clippers. Where are those clippers? You waste an hour looking for it, only to find it under the sink. It is now noon and is too hot to go outside. You set this chore aside for another day.

Does that situation sound familiar? Having to hunt for items kills one's productivity. By decluttering and organizing your home, you will save a lot of time looking for things that you need. Experts in home organization say that having things where they need to be can boost your productivity. Plus, the process of cleaning is actually an energy booster. So, you get more energy to do the things that you need simply by spending a few minutes a day putting back things where they should be.

Spring Cleaning Can Improve Your Health

While everybody is rejoicing for the coming of spring, some people dread this time of the year. Yes, I am talking about people who have various seasonal allergies. Tree pollens and molds are prevalent during this period. Going outside is very difficult for people who are sensitive to these.

Unfortunately, staying indoors may not be the best option for allergy sufferers either. Dust and grime can trigger many people's allergies as well. Based on a study conducted by the American College of Allergy, Asthma, and Immunology, doing a deep clean every year can drastically improve your health, particularly if you suffer from any allergies.

By getting rid of things that are falling apart and giving your carpet a nice wash and vacuum, you will feel much healthier. No more watery eyes, congestion, uncontrollable sneezing, and itchy nose, mouth, and throat.

Spring Cleaning Can Boost Your Mood

Some individuals experience what is known as seasonal affective disorder (SAD). This is a type of depression that is brought on by the lack of exposure to sunlight. The body's daily rhythm is disrupted, and people experience irritability, a marked decrease in energy, and craving for starchy or sugary food. One way of combating this is going outside. Another is to be more active. If you combine being active with doing something productive, such as doing spring cleaning, then you can boost your mood exponentially.

Spring Cleaning Can Lessen Your Stress

Clutter has been proven to make a person feel bad. Those strewn toys on the floor, bills and other paper left unorganized on the table, and endless containers of leftover food that has been "marinating" in the fridge for months can take a toll on one's health and mood.

Besides the stress, clutter can also take a toll on one's self-esteem. Having a dirty home may be viewed as laziness on the part of the homeowner. Finally, studies have linked clutter to one's tendency to get distracted. The more clutter there is around a person, the more you tend to lose your focus.

By doing a deep clean of your house, you will be able to address the clutter once and for all (or at least for the next few weeks). Clearing up your floor, cabinets, and refrigerator is very therapeutic. The less clutter there is, the more focus you can put into important things that need doing. Plus, you don't have to waste so much time sifting through trash to get to the item that you need. Additionally, you can invite guests over again.

Set Your Cleaning Calendar

For any project to succeed, it is important to have a plan. You need to have a list of tasks that you want to accomplish during this cleaning frenzy period. If you have a list, you are less likely to forget to do something important. Equally important is to set a date for this particular project.

Remember, this is not something that you can accomplish in a day. Although the goal of this book is to have you go through the entire thing in a short time, it is important to note that you might not want to limit yourself to just 30 minutes a day for this particular project. Some people will want to spend hours cleaning.

The first thing to look at is your appointment calendar. Choose a week that you know is a slow one for you. Do not schedule any major projects when you expect to be busy at work (or are preparing for a huge exam in school). If you are doing the cleaning project with other people in the house, it is crucial to consider their schedules as well.

Some cleaning experts claim that scheduling your spring cleaning while it is still a little bit cold outside is advisable. That way, when it is truly warm and sunny, you will be able to enjoy the weather rather than be cooped up cleaning your windows.

Block out this week and mark it as "Spring Cleaning" on your calendar/s. You will most likely be doing some heavy lifting or scrubbing at this time, so scheduling a get-together with your friends in the middle of this week might not be ideal.

Create Your Task List

There are many ways to create a task list for your spring-cleaning project. You can do it per day or per room. What we will be doing in this book is assigning a room per day. In your "itinerary" you would want to write down all the tasks that you want to finish during this period. Be as detailed as possible.

If you commit to doing everything on the list, you will have fewer excuses to back down once the cleaning frenzy begins. Below is just a small part of the spring-cleaning task list that you might want to work with. Later on, you will be provided with a more comprehensive cleaning task list per room.

- Vacuum the floor
- Wipe the wall and ceiling
- Put throw rugs in the hamper
- Wash windows and mirrors
- Spray and soak the floor (for tiled floors)
- Rinse the floor and mop dry

Besides the regular cleaning tasks, include a list of cleaning goals that you really want to accomplish during this period. This way, you will know which tasks to prioritize. If you do run out of steam or time, at least you'd have done the most important tasks for you. Examples of priority goals are:

- Weeding out books from your collection – If you are running out of shelf space for your new books, it might be time to weed out some of the books that you do not plan on rereading.

- Deep clean the bathroom – If your bathroom grout is already looking very yellow (or gray), this might be something that you would want to prioritize.

- Get rid of mold under the sink – Anything that is growing inside your home (whether it is insects or molds) should be prioritized. Molds not only look gross, but they can also cause health problems.

Get Your Cleaning Kit Ready

Before you embark on your cleaning project it is important to get everything that you will need ready and in one place. Your plan can get easily derailed when, right before you are scheduled to clean your windows, you discover that you do not have any glass cleaner. Taking a trip to the store to get a forgotten item will kill your momentum, and probably dampen your enthusiasm for the project.

Do you get intimidated by the number of cleaning products that you see in home improvement aisles? That's normal. Manufacturers come up with so many products and tools designed to keep your home clean and disinfected.

The truth is, you won't need most of those items during your spring cleaning. Having just the basics should suffice. Here is a list of products that you must prepare to ensure that your spring-cleaning project goes smoothly. Keep these in a handy caddy (or a bucket) so that you can easily move all of them from one room to the other.

- All-purpose cleaner – whether it is to remove the stains on your floor or to get that food oil off the stove, an all-purpose cleaner is a very helpful product to have when you are cleaning. Regular dishwashing liquid can be a good alternative if you don't have this readily.

- Dishwashing liquid – this is the best cleaner for the job when it comes to getting rid of grease.

- Detergent – This is essential when you need to clean and disinfect surfaces and fabrics.

- Oven-cleaner – for greasy jobs, you might need to use something a little bit stronger than regular soap. This is where this specialized product comes in. Many homeowners claim that this can be replaced with a mixture of baking soda and white vinegar.

- Glass-cleaner – to remove streaks, nothing beats a good glass-cleaner for your windows and mirrors.

Here Are the Tools That You Will Need Too:

- Vacuum
- Spray bottle
- Floor mop
- Broom
- Scrubbing sponges
- Microfiber cloth
- Rags
- Bucket
- Grout brush
- Toilet brush
- Rubber gloves

Having these items on hand will ensure that your cleaning process goes without a hitch. If you are planning on doing a major decluttering, having some boxes or durable garbage bags will also be beneficial. You will need them for the things that you would like to store or deliver to the dump or a donation drop-off.

Chapter 2 – Day 1: Start Small and Slow

We understand that you have been inactive for the most part of the winter. Don't go straining yourself by doing a lot of heavy lifting on the first day of your spring-cleaning project. It is best if you do it slowly. Once you have a few tasks done, then you can move on to bigger and more energy-consuming chores.

The first thing that you need to do is to look at your plan. Where will you start? What things should you have in your cleaning kit? By having a clear idea of the number of tasks that you have to undertake, you'll be able to tell yourself that this project is not insurmountable. You know that there is an end. Familiarize yourself with the cleaning products that you will use if this is the first time that you will be using them.

Set Out the Boxes for Things That You Will Sort

Many home organization experts suggest that you set out 4 boxes for the things that you will pick up:

- Keep – this box is for the things that you want to keep but are not in their proper place
- Sell/Donate – this box is for the items that are still usable but no longer serve a purpose in your life
- Store – this box is for the items that you will not use in the near future
- Trash – this is for things that you can no longer fix or donate.

Instead of keeping a box of trash, just tip the object directly into the wastebasket. Do not spend more time sorting through garbage. This will only give you an opportunity to put it back on the shelf.

Dust Every Surface

Dust doesn't stop forming even during winter. Dusting is not something that you can get away from. You will see in the coming chapters that you will have to do it more extensively per room. For the first day though, bring out the dust rag and give everything that you pass a quick swipe.

For people who suffer from allergies to dust or dirt, it is a good idea to wear a mask now. For those who get itchy when they encounter dust, it might be handy to keep a spray bottle filled with a mixture of water and surface cleaner (the kind that you don't have to rinse off) with you. If you spray the surface with this solution, you will be able to pick up dust with your rag without it getting all over your skin.

Pick Up Visible Clutter

Go through each room quickly and pick up items that shouldn't be there in the first place. Just deal with the things that you can readily see. Do not "unearth" clutter. This is just the first pass anyway. Place these items in the Keep box. After going through all the rooms (or each room, if you prefer), empty the box by putting back the items in their rightful place. And by rightful place, its either back on the shelf or drawer where they should be or in the trash bin.

Call in The Experts

If you need to have your carpet shampooed or your air-conditioning unit serviced, now is the time to call in the professionals. They should be able to do the maintenance tasks before you get to clean the rooms where the items belong to. This way, you don't get dust or debris on the floors that you already mopped and vacuumed.

Chapter 3 – Day 2: Tackle the Dreaded Bathroom

Now that you have a few tasks under your belt, you might be inspired enough to take on a bigger project. It is time to tackle the bathroom. Most homeowners dread cleaning their bathrooms because they'd have to deal with removing hair from their drains or scrubbing gunk from their grout. But, once you have this done, all other tasks would seem so much easier.

You might be wondering if this would really only take 30 minutes of your day. The truth is, if you have neglected this room, it will take you more than half an hour to get it in order. But, once the heavy lifting has been done, you will only need a few minutes each week to keep it in pristine condition.

Here is a list of things to do to get your bathroom to sparkle and shine once more:

- Remove any items that do not belong in this room.
- Dust light fixtures.
- Wash the walls and the baseboards
- Clean doors and doorknobs
- Wipe switch plates
- Wash windows/screens
- Check the batteries of your smoke detector
- Clean the tub
- Scrub the sink
- Deep clean the floor
- Wash the mats and rugs
- Clean and disinfect the toilet
- Clean the waste bin
- Clean the shower heads
- Replace shower curtains
- Wipe down the shower rings and rod
- Organize and clean out medicine cabinet/vanity
- Shine the mirror
- Organize and clean out the linen closet

- Do an inventory of your bathroom supplies (soap, shampoo, etc.)

Organize Your Medicine Cabinet or Bathroom Drawer

While some cleaning experts advise that you leave the cleaning of these cabinets for last, it might actually make more sense if you do this task first. This way, if you spill any medicine or accidentally drop something dusty, you wouldn't need to scrub your sink or floor all over again. Get rid of all the items that are not supposed to be inside the bathroom.

Place them back in their rightful place or throw them away. Check each and every bottle in your medicine cabinet. Get rid of any medicine or product that is past its expiration date. Give the drawers and medicine cabinet a quick wipe down before putting back the items that you took out.

Clean the Wastebasket in Your Bathroom

This task would be super easy if you use a bin liner for the wastebasket in your bathroom. All you would need to do is to change and replace the liner once a week.

If you don't use a bin liner, then your task has gotten a little more complicated. First, empty the wastebasket. Set it down in under the sink or the shower. Spray it with water. Turn the basket over so it would dry better. Make sure that you do this step before you start cleaning your floor.

Clean and Disinfect All the Surfaces

One of the yuckiest tasks to do in this room is to clean the tile and grout in the bathing area. This can easily get gunky if you don't give it a good scrub from time to time. If your bathroom tiles already have mold, you might need to call in a professional to address that problem. However, if they are just dirty, all you need is to let the cleaning solution soak for a few minutes and then scrub off the dirt with a good brush.

Fill your spray bottle with the right combination of all-purpose cleaner and water. Spray the tiles and grout with the solution. Use a plastic brush to scrub off the dirt that has built up on the surface. Rinse the area with water. Spraying the cleaning solution is faster than using a rag to apply the cleaning solution.

Plus, you don't have to touch any yucky surface. Do the same for the vanity or sink and the upper part of the toilet. You can also spray the floor and walls of the bathroom. You can use a mop to work the product onto the surface. Rinse everything with water then mop the floor again.

You can also create your own cleaning concoction by combining ¼ cup of white vinegar, some lemon juice (or lemon essential oil), and a few drops of dish detergent. Put this in your spray bottle and fill it with water

Get Rid of Mildew with Baking Soda Paste

Because the room is always wet, water spots and mildew can form. You can get rid of these by scrubbing the area using an old toothbrush and baking soda paste. You can make the paste by combining baking soda and water. You can also use this paste for cleaning the sink fixtures and drain block.

Clean and Disinfect the Toilet Thoroughly

Most people just ignore doing this task until a ring of discoloration starts forming in the toilet bowl. You can prevent this scum ring from forming by doing a weekly clean-up. However, if it is already there, just use your baking soda paste to get rid of the stains on your toilet.

Use the old toothbrush to apply the paste all over the toilet, particularly under the rim. Let it soak for a few minutes before scrubbing it off. You can also drop two antacid tablets (or the tablets that some people use to clean their dentures) into the bowl to disinfect it. Let it soak overnight before flushing it. Make sure to keep the lid closed.

After this, do weekly maintenance to keep the toilet from getting too dirty. You can do this by pouring a cleaning mixture around the bowl of the toilet before you take a bath. You can make your own cleaning mixture using 1/8 cup of white vinegar and a few drops of tea tree oil.

Wash The Bath Mats And Rugs

Because they are always moist, the mats and rugs in your bathroom will likely grow musty or moldy. Additionally, they will probably pick up dust, residue, and hair. This is why it is important to give these a good wash.

To prevent your bath rug from getting moldy, make sure that it is thoroughly dry before putting it down. Letting it dry under the sun will also ensure that bacteria gets killed. You will know that you did not properly dry out your rug because it will start smelling funky a few days after you place it in your bathroom.

Chapter 4 – Day 3: Deep Clean the Kitchen and the Dining Room

The kitchen is one place that you need to keep clean. This is where you prepare your food. You don't want to get sick because you cooked your food someplace that is not in the best shape. So, it is time to deal with that musty refrigerator, greasy oven, and cluttered kitchen cabinets.

If you are looking at your kitchen right now and wondering, "Will this only take me 30 minutes to clean?" The answer will actually depend on how diligent you were in keeping this room, and the adjacent dining room, clean and uncluttered during your hibernation period.

If you regularly got rid of food packaging and gave your counter a wipe down whenever you cooked something, you won't have to worry too much about taking long in cleaning this room. If you've neglected it, then you might take a little over an hour. Still, taking a few hours of your third day will all be worth it once you see your kitchen drawers in perfect order and everything on your kitchen counter gleaming.

Here is a list of things to do to get your kitchen back in tip-top shape:

- Remove any items that do not belong in this room.
- Dust light fixtures.
- Dust down the corner of walls and ceiling.
- Wipe the walls and the baseboards with a damp cloth
- Clean doors and doorknobs
- Wipe switch plates
- Wash windows/screens
- Check the batteries of your smoke detector
- Take down the curtains for washing / wash the dust off the blinds
- Wash the dish drainer, microwave turntable, pans, bowls, and dishes
- Clean the countertops and stovetop
- Deep clean the oven
- Empty and clean the refrigerator
- Empty and dust the shelves (pantry)
- Wipe down cabinets and microwave
- Wipe down appliances

- Empty and clean all the drawers
- Organize your kitchenware
- Empty the sink and wipe it down
- Empty the trash and clean the wastebasket
- Vacuum under the dining table
- Give your dining chairs and table a good wipe down
- Mop the floor

Inspect the Walls and Other Surfaces for Food Debris

The kitchen is one place where splatter is common. It may be necessary to spot wash some parts of the wall to remove any food debris or grease. You can use the same cleaning solution that you used for the bathroom. Spray the area that needs cleaning, rub it using a rag, then give the area a wipe down using a damp cloth.

Wash Your Kitchen Curtains And Table Cloth

Grease can build up in the fibers of the fabrics that you have in your kitchen area. To get rid of this, you will need to give the curtains and table cloth a good wash. Once you have taken down the curtain or blinds, make sure that you vacuum the windowsill. Wash the windows and clean the glass with a good glass cleaner. Make sure that everything is dry before placing the fabrics back.

Clean Your Kitchen Appliances Based on The Manufacturer's Instructions

Use a good oven cleaner for your oven. Follow the instructions that come with the cleaner. Make sure that the kitchen is well ventilated when you do this. While you are waiting for the oven cleaner to do its job, clean the other kitchen appliances. Unplug your kitchen appliances and vacuum the area behind and underneath each. Make sure to wipe the cables and coils clean using a damp cloth.

As for big appliances, move them aside so you can vacuum and sweep the dust that has built up underneath. Wipe the exteriors of the small appliances. For the microwave, make sure that the interior is free from food debris before plugging it back in. For fossilized food debris, steam it off by boiling a cup of water in the microwave. To remove any bad smells, boil a cup of water with some lemon juice in it. Run the dishwasher while it is empty. Clean out the food trap and give the exterior a good wipe down.

Deep Clean the Stove by Degreasing the Surface

Your stove can easily get greasy even if you wipe the surface every time you finish cooking. To clean this thoroughly, get all the burners and put them in the sink. Make a mixture of dishwashing liquid and lukewarm water. Wash off the greasy film on the burners. Rinse thoroughly. Make your baking soda paste (water and baking soda) and coat the burners.

Leave this on for 15 minutes. You can do your other tasks as the baking soda works its magic. Scrub off the baking soda paste and softened food debris. Spray the stove panel with all-purpose cleaner (or the vinegar/lemon mixture that you prepared for the bathroom). Wipe off the liquid completely. This should deal with the greasy build-up on the stove.

Go Through Every Item in Your Refrigerator and Pantry

Sort through the food and other items inside the refrigerator. Before doing that, fill your sink with soapy water. Check for empty or nearly empty containers inside the fridge. Dump the food debris and place the container in the sink. Throw out any items that have turned or is past its expiry date. Keep the stuff that you will still eat or cook on the counter. Once the fridge has been emptied out, take out the shelves and drawers and wash those in the sink.

Give the interior and exterior of your fridge a good wipe down with soapy water. Wipe the soap off afterward. Give the surface another wipe-down using a clean rag to get rid of the soap. Dry the newly washed shelves before putting them back. Replace the food items. It is important that you do this as quickly as possible to prevent your food from going bad.

Do the same for the shelves of your pantry. Remove the food items that are no longer edible and give the shelves a good wipe down. If needed, use the vacuum to remove any tiny food debris left behind. If you can, line the cabinets before putting back the things that you took out. This would make it easier to clean the pantry next time.

Deep Clean Your Sink and Garbage Disposal System

Once you are done washing everything that needs to be washed, clean the sink. Pour some baking soda down the garbage disposal to ensure that it is clean. To remove any odor, run the garbage disposal then allow a few lemon peels to go through it. You might also want to drop a few ice cubes down the disposal. This will sharpen the blades. Wipe down the sink.

Chapter 5 – Day 4: Make your Living Room Lively Once More

Besides the kitchen and the dining room, the living room is another most used space in the house. Thus, it can easily get dirty and cluttered. The good news is that there shouldn't be any grimy or greasy build up to deal with in this area. You will be doing a lot of dusting and vacuuming in this room.

The bad news is that this room tends to accumulate the most amount of clutter. It is best to prepare a container where you can place all the things that shouldn't be in the living room. As you clean the space, pick up the wayward items and place them in the box. Once you are done cleaning, you can start sorting through the items in the box and begin putting them back in their proper places.

Here is a list of things to do to make your living room lively once more:

- Remove any items that do not belong in this room.

- Dust light fixtures.
- Dust down the corner of walls and ceiling.
- Dust down the electronics (unplug them first)
- Wipe the walls and the baseboards with a damp cloth
- Clean doors and doorknobs
- Wipe switch plates
- Wash windows/screens
- Check the batteries of your smoke detector
- Take down the curtains for washing / wash the dust off the blinds
- Vacuum the couch
- Remove the covers of the throw pillows and slipcovers for washing
- Remove the items on the coffee table and dust it down
- Vacuum the floor and the carpet

Dust Down Everything

Grab your duster and remove the dust from the ceiling, wall corners, shelves, air vents, and other surfaces. Carefully dust all the photographs, art, and other decorations in the room. If you have a ceiling fan, don't forget to dust that. If possible, take it down for a good wash. Dry everything before putting it back up. Use a dry duster to clean light fixtures.

Wash the Draperies, Curtains, And Screens

Take down the curtains and draperies and put them in the wash. While it is washing and drying, vacuum the windowsills. Clean the glass on the windows using a good glass cleaner. Use the microfiber rag to wipe off the cleaner. If you have mosquito screens installed, take this down for washing. Make sure that they are completely dry before reinstalling on your windows to avoid rusting.

Remove the Dust from Your Couch and Chairs

Before vacuuming your couch, make sure that there are no important items trapped in its crevices. Carefully run your fingers through the space to see. You might be surprised by the number of items that you might find trapped in there.

Once the couch has been cleared of any important stuff, vacuum the entire thing. Do the same for the other chairs in the room. If there are any stains on the couch, use a spot cleaner to remove it. Place the slipcovers, and accent pillows in the wash.

Purge Your Bookshelves

Remove all the books and items from your bookshelves. Give the shelves a good wipe down. Replace only the books that you want to keep. Place the other books and old magazines in the box that you have designated for items for donation. As for the knickknacks that you use as decoration, wipe those down using a damp cloth before placing them back on the shelves.

Deep Clean the Rugs and Carpets

Carpets are dust magnets. Make sure that this, along with other rugs in the room, is thoroughly dusted using a vacuum. For heavily soiled carpets, you can rent one of those special cleaning machines that can remove deep-seated grime. You can also bring it to a carpet cleaner for professional cleaning. Make sure to sweep and vacuum the floor thoroughly before replacing the carpet.

For rubber or plastic doormats, vacuuming may not be enough. Take those outside and give them a good wash with detergent and water. The same goes for your heavily-soiled fabric rugs. For rugs made from natural fibers, consult the cleaning instructions that came with it before doing anything.

Polish Your Wooden Furniture

For that extra oomph, it might be ideal to polish your wooden furniture. Make sure that these are free from dust before applying the polish. Use a soft cloth for this step. You can also make your own furniture polish that you can pour into a spray bottle. Just mix one-part white vinegar and four parts olive oil. Spray this onto the wooden surface and buff it until it shines.

Chapter 6 – Day 5: Turn your Bedroom Back into a Restful Haven

Sleep is very important. The quality of your sleep can have a huge impact on the quality of your waking hours. One way to improve the quality of your sleep is to make sure that your bedroom is clean. The coming of spring is the perfect time to check if your bedroom is the sleep sanctuary that you deserve or is it keeping you up all night.

The most important part of going through this room is cleaning the bed. If this is the only thing that you can do in the 30 minutes that you allotted, then you may have done 80% of the job.

Here is a list of things to do to make your bedroom a restful haven:

- Remove any items that do not belong in this room.
- Dust light fixtures.
- Dust down the corner of walls and ceiling.
- Wipe the walls and the baseboards with a damp cloth

- Clean doors and doorknobs
- Wipe switch plates
- Wash windows/screens
- Check the batteries of your smoke detector
- Take down the curtains for washing / wash the dust off the blinds
- Dust the ceiling fan
- Remove all the beddings and put them in the wash
- Vacuum the windowsill
- Polish all glass surfaces
- Wipe down lamps
- Wipe down the bed frame
- Vacuum the mattress
- Flip the mattress if necessary
- Mop then vacuum the floor
- Clean the carpet

Put Everything That Doesn't Belong in Your Bedroom in A Bag or Box

Weird objects tend to end up either in or under the bed. Go ahead and check yours out now. You will find shoes, recipe books, spoons, and tools there. Your bed (and your bedroom) should be a sanctuary meant for sleeping.

So, it is a must to remove anything that can interrupt your sleep from this area. Place all the wayward things in a box or bag. Once you are done cleaning your bedroom, check your box and assess where the found things really need to be.

Get Your Bed Ready for Warmer Weather

Strip off all the heavy flannel beddings and replace them with airier ones. Pack away the extra blankets after washing because you won't be needing them for a while. Before putting on newly washed sheets, make sure that you flip the mattress.

This will allow your mattress to resettle and make it last longer. Wash your pillows based on the manufacturer's instructions. If they are already old, consider getting new pillows. Make sure that washed beddings are fully dried before putting them back on the bed. Moist beddings can harbor molds. The same is true for curtains.

Deep Clean Your Humidifier

Moldy humidifiers can actually do more harm than good. Deep clean your humidifier by scrubbing its insides with a solution of vinegar and water. You can also use hydrogen peroxide if you have that on hand.

Deep Clean Your Wood Furniture

If you have a wooden bed frame, side table, and multimedia console in your bedroom, now is the perfect time to deep clean them. First off, make sure that their surfaces are free of dust. Give the furniture a good wipe down with a damp cloth. If you have applied polish on the furniture in the past, you might need to remove that first before reapplying wax. The buildup of product can make your furniture sticky.

Remember the vinegar-and-water solution that you poured into a spray bottle? You can use that for this room too. Just spray the wood and wipe off with a clean rag. You might have to do this several times if the wax is applied pretty thick. Once the buildup has been removed, let the furniture dry for a few minutes. You can then apply a new coating of wax. Follow the manufacturer's instructions for proper application steps.

Organize the Bedside Table

Your bedside table should only contain the things that you need when you are already in bed. It shouldn't have snacks, stacks of books, or your old utility bills on it. Dust everything using a damp cloth. Don't spray your framed art or photographs as the liquid might damage the picture.

Chapter 7 – Day 6: Declutter your Shelves, Cabinets, and Closets

Closets and cabinets are very hard to deal with when doing a deep clean of the house. They usually look clean from the outside. However, once you open it, you will discover that it has been filled to the brim with things that you no longer use but are not willing to dispose of yet, or things that you still use but cannot get to because it has been pinned under other things.

Having an organized closet or cabinet (or even shelves) doesn't require you to buy all the latest organization tool in the market. All you need to have is a clear plan on where the items should go. A few bins and boxes will definitely help but they are not necessary if you simply want to clean these parts of the house.

Here is a list of things to do to organize your closet, cabinets, and shelves:

- Throw out all the trash (carriers, old paper bags, tags from clothes).
- Gather all the clean clothes. Sort them: for hanging, for folding.
- Hang all the clothes that would wrinkle.
- Fold all the clothes that would not wrinkle.
- Vacuum the space that you cleared out.
- Wipe down the surfaces using a microfiber cloth.
- Dust all the knickknacks and decorations
- Clean your shoes.

Sort Your Clothes

When sorting your clothes, don't be too critical and start sorting them according to fabric or color. This would take longer. Start with making two piles: for hanging and for folding. This will enable you to go through all your clothes in just minutes. Once you have everything sorted out and placed back in your closet, you can go back and do a more customized sorting.

The items that you would normally hang are:

- Skirts
- Dresses

- Robes
- Slacks
- Blouses
- Jackets or blazers

The items that you would normally fold are:

- Shorts
- Jeans
- Sweatshirts/sweatpants
- T-shirts
- Underwear
- Socks

Do Not Dump Out the Entire Closet

Most people would jump right in and pull out all the items in the closet. While this makes sense, some people tend to run out of time or steam during the cleaning process. If this happens, you will be forced to cram everything that you took out right back into the space. It might make more sense if you work on the closet one shelf or drawer at a time.

- Clear out the space.
- Vacuum the space to get rid of any dust. Keep an eye out for small things such as jewelry or any other trinket.

- Give the surface a good wipe down with a damp cloth, let it dry as you organize the items that you took out.
- Think of a logical way to put back the things that you took out.
- Put back everything in their rightful places
- Move on to the next shelf or drawer.

Weed Out the Items That You No Longer Want or Need

Once you have a more organized closet, you can better see the things that are inside it. This is the time to remove any object inside it that you no longer need or want. Now, this can be an emotional move for some people. You don't have to do it unless you really are ready for this step. Create three piles of things to be weeded out of your closet, cabinet, or shelf:

1. Dispose pile: Clothing and other items that are already too worn out to be repaired or donated.
2. Donate pile: Items that are still usable but you no longer want to keep.
3. Store pile: Items that you will not use now but will use eventually (winter clothes, clothes that are still good but doesn't fit you).

For the dispose pile, think of ways for you to be able to repurpose the items. Maybe cut them up and use the fabric for your other sewing projects? You can also use these items as rags for future cleaning.

As for the store pile, make sure that you place the items in clearly marked bins before putting them in your storage space.

Do the same for other items like art pieces, decorations, books, etc. If you want to keep them, dust them off and place them back. If you want to get rid of them, either place them in the dispose pile or the donate pile.

Clean Your Shoe Before Putting Them Back in The Closet or Shoe Cabinet

Grab a brush and go outside for this step. Brush off any dirt from the bottoms of your shoes. Treat your shoes based on the material.

- Leather shoes – Remove any stains using the vinegar and water solution. Buff the surface with a clean, soft rag.

- Patent leather shoes – Apply petroleum jelly on scuff marks using cotton swabs. Spray the surface with some glass cleaner to bring back its shine.

- Suede shoes – Buff stains off by scrubbing the surface with a soft brush.

- Canvass shoes – Whiten the soles by applying baking soda paste on the surface. Toss the shoes in the washing machine and use the gentle cycle for this. Make sure that you only use half the prescribed amount of soap for one wash. Air dry.

- Rubber shoes – Treat stains with a mixture of detergent and water. Apply the soap using an old toothbrush. Use a damp sponge to remove the suds. Wash the laces in the washing machine together with the canvass shoes.

Chapter 8 – Day 7: Final Pass and Trip to the Donation Place/ Recycling center / Dump

Okay, you have done the heavy lifting, dusting, scrubbing, and wiping. Before you declare this spring-cleaning project as done, it is important to go over every room to see if you have indeed finished doing all the tasks.

Check for Any Leftover Clutter

Inspect each and every room. You might be surprised to see a few items that have escaped your first and second pass. Grab those things and quickly put them in their rightful place.

Do A Final Pass with Your Vacuum?

For any leftover dust balls, clumps of hair, or crumbs that you may have missed, it is important that you go over the surfaces with your trusty vacuum.

Spot Clean Any Stains That You Missed

Keep a stain removing pen or spray bottle handy so you can quickly spot clean any dirt or stain that you may have missed. This is where your caddy will really help. If you have your cleaning kit with you, you can easily deal with these wayward stains and not be compelled to leave them for your next cleaning spree.

Wash the Rags That You Used

Don't forget that your dirty rags, mats, gloves, etc. will also need washing after you are done cleaning. If they are beyond help, you might opt to toss them in the trash can. However, for dusty rags, just throw them in the washing machine, add a few scoopfuls of detergent, and wash them. Hang them to dry before putting them back where you store your cleaning supplies.

Gather the Things That You Want to Donate, Recycle, Or Throw Away

Don't stop now. Get the boxes of items for donation, recycling, and for throwing away. Drop them off at the appropriate centers as soon as possible. This way, you won't have the opportunity to go through them again and decide that you still want to keep that old unicorn costume that no longer fits you and you can't possibly use anymore.

Conclusion

Spring cleaning is not an easy task. If it were, you will not need this guide book to help you out. It can be tedious, tiring, and emotionally taxing. But the reward is not just having a cleaner house that you can be proud of. You will also get peace of mind, knowing that you have seen everything in your house and have gotten rid of everything that you don't use, don't need, or can't fix.

This means everything is in good shape for the next few months (at the very least). With each item back in their proper place, you can start working on your other projects with ease. Plus, you get to rid yourself of the lethargy that comes with being cooped up inside for weeks on end.

Now, since you have already put in the effort of doing a massive clean-up, all that is left to do is to keep the house from getting unnecessarily and excessively dirty once more. Even five minutes of upkeep per day will make a huge difference. Keep clutter at a minimum. Wipe the surfaces after they have been used. You will have an easier time during your next spring cleaning if you prevent grime and clutter from building up.

Printed in Great Britain
by Amazon

24193317R00037